# Conversations
# & Poetry

## MICHAEL R. MILANO

**FCP**

*Full Court Press*
*Englewood Cliffs, New Jersey*

Published in the United States of America
by Full Court Press, 601 Palisade Avenue
Englewood Cliffs, NJ 07632

"Minimalism" previously appeared in *The Abbey*, and "I
Became a Doctor," "Memento Mori," and "Hearing" in *The
Pharos*, for which the author acknowledges his gratitude.

ISBN 978-0-9846113-4-8
Library of Congress Control No. 2010936368

*Cover Image, "Piet-y," by Michael R. Milano
Editing, Book Design, and Author Photograph
by Barry Sheinkopf for Bookshapers (www.bookshapers.com)
Colophon by Liz Sedlack*

To My Mother
Mary Bottiglieri Milano

# Table of Contents

## PART FOUR: MEDICAL POEMS

## PART FIVE: ART

## PART SIX: HUMOR

# Introduction

M Y FIRST POETRY WORKSHOP leader discouraged me from seeking publication until I had completed thirty poems, enough to counter the inevitable rejections. Well, here are all thirty, including the four published, and acknowledged on the copyright page. A bonus is prose and poetry from Pat. I wanted to collect my poems and try to discover whether they could be distinguished by themes. Yes, there were themes, and they have been loosely organized by chapters.

I also like to talk about poems, both their meaning and their structure. It is not poetic to explain one's own poetry, but the commentary may be more interesting than the poems. Hence the title, Conversations and Poetry. At the least, I hope the practice makes the poems more reader friendly. A little less struggle about meaning allows more enjoyment of the words themselves. Where they come from, what they mean, and how they are put together has not been always clear to readers (or me, at times). Jon Long, our opera singer friend, reads them slowly and with an element of theater. If you like a poem, mine or anyone else's, read it aloud and with maximum emphasis. This works especially well with shorter poems and rhymed ones.

The collection represents the contributions of many people. Pat has been my major reader, and Betty Carpenter my amanuensis. Our poetry reading group, Bob, Addie, Jeff, Jon, and Pat, got me started writing and have made stimulating suggestions throughout. They have supported the idea that poetry is important. It is. Further editorial assistance has come from Bob Ghirardella, Jon Long, and Barry Sheinkopf. They have helped me immeasurably.

If everyone has one book in them, this is mine.

# Part One: Whitehall

*Where else could I begin? Most of my readers know the stories about Whitehall, but a love note to my home town would be an obvious start. Whitehall was a small pond but a rich one. I lament the exclusion from the book of Doc Wheeler's ice wagon and ice house, the Valastro's sandlot baseball, the playground, Sabo Sabo's pool hall, the Blue Goose, and so many aunts and uncles, too soon gone. They are the Whitehall treasures that haven't yet become poems. Let's start with a memoir, a nostalgic literal map to Whitehall, written by Pat around 1970.*

## PAT'S WHITEHALL

Almost from our first date, Mike started telling me about his hometown, Whitehall, New York , and the two strong women in his life—his mother, Mary, and his aunt Irene. The town lies ninety miles north of Albany, at the base of Lake Champlain. It had once been a flourishing industrial center with silk mills going twenty-four hours a day and railroads and canals for transport. But all of that ended after the war, and by 1959, when I got there, time had been standing still for many years. I experienced Whitehall's small-town intimacy and unchanging ways as an almost mystical haven, which I fell in love with, along with its favorite son.

The first time I was driven to Whitehall by my college beau bringing me home to meet his family, we took a puzzle of connecting two-lane state roads. In our self-preoccupation we failed to notice a sign that said Entering Lake George Village, Speed Limit 25 M.P.H. and sailed right into the local revenue farmers slamming fifty dollar fines on all out-of-towners as they crossed the town line. The news of this reached Whitehall before we did. "Michael," his mother said before she had even met me, "you should have been paying more attention." Next to her stood Aunt Irene roguishly making the shame sign with her fingers. News traveled fast since there was so little of it. Now, when we make the trip, we take the quadruple lanes of the Interstate Northway that stretches from Albany to Montreal, bypassing Saratoga, Glens Falls, Fort Edward, and other towns whose Main Streets used to be our homeward route. Sixty-five is legal, and seventy is fine if it's dry. One hour out of Albany, we leave the Northway for the Fort Ann Road.

Once I asked Mike if he knew the name of the road we were on; he replied, "The Fort Ann Road."

"No it isn't," his smart aleck passenger quipped. "It's the 'Farm to Market Road.' Says so on the sign."

"Well, it may say so on the sign, but there isn't a person around here who would know what you were talking about if you called it that."

From Fort Ann we pick up Route 22 and follow the Old Barge Canal. It's a treacherous two-lane road on which I've never had the nerve to pass so much as a Volkswagon Beetle and usually struggle for miles stuck behind a farm truck. But Mike knows the road like the back of his hand and always makes good time. He should. His grandfather, Nicholas Bottiglieri, was the *padrone* responsible for bringing the Italian immigrant laborers to Whitehall to build the canal.

The landmarks rush out to greet us as we speed along. Porky's Diner Just Over the Hill, the billboard reads. Sad to say, Porky's Diner went over the hill eight years before: the first change I witnessed after starting to visit Whitehall. The sign has never been taken down, and at the crest of the hill I still expect to see the trucks pulled up in front of Porky's. We pass another sign for The Whitehall Drive Inn, a cow pasture with a movie screen that operates on Saturday night in the summer. Then a sign that says Whitehall, New York, Birthplace of the United States Navy, a bit of folklore burnished by the town's various historians, Mike's mother among them, based on the fact that the American Army built a ship here, the Ticonderoga, during the Revolutionary War. The black and rotted hulk which claimed to be the skeleton of that ship has recently been dignified with a sheltering roof and a sign explaining its significance.

Route 22 becomes Broadway once in Whitehall. We'll pass Newell's car dealership, where Mike's mother once worked until the mechanics complained that she was always telling them how to make repairs. She probably did, and I have no doubt she knew more than they did. Walt Newell is the town rake—has been for years—but his wife Rose doesn't seem to mind, and all agree he is very good to his family. We'll pass Uncle Tony Siraco's gas station, one of the twenty-two in the little village whose population when we visit will swell to 3,800. Then we will pass Uncle Tony and Aunt Madeleine's house, with grottoes and flamingoes in the front yard, and next door, his liquor store. The second change I saw in White-hall came when Uncle Tony put up the neon sign over his liquor store that spells

L-I-Q-U-O-R and flashes arrows toward the store below. As there is only one other liquor store in town, this attention-getter seems superfluous, but Uncle Tony must have felt his customers deserved some spectacle for their loyal patronage.

Across the street from Uncle Tony's little empire is the "Irish church," a misnomer that distinguishes it from the other Catholic church in town, the "French church." When I visit I am just about the only Irishman, since both congregations are close to a hundred percent Italian. Mike's father was buried from the Irish church six years before I first came to Whitehall. And it was from the Irish church that Noni, Mike's grandmother, was buried the week before our engagement would have been announced. It was delayed because Mike, his mother, and his aunt Irene were in mourning for a woman who had been bedridden for eight years, the last four of them aphasic. The only sound she could make was a "babababa" type of ululation. Yet, like a new baby, she had been the center of the house with every member of the family paying attention to her and all the neighbors stopping in to visit her from time to time. They'd tell her some gossip or a funny joke they'd heard. She loved risque' stories and was said to have had a fantastic repertoire of them. She was never viewed as a burden. At her funeral the Ladies of Mt. Carmel, not one of whom weighed less than two hundred pounds, walked behind her hearse for a mile from the Irish church to the cemetery.

Just past the church is the family homestead where Mike was raised. Irene and her family live downstairs, and Mary has her apartment upstairs. Irene married late in life, and in the years before she had her own children Mike was her sidekick. She took over running the family's grocery store next door when her father died. She can butcher a side of beef or tell you how to shake up a pint basket of strawberries to make it look full. She is a big, strong woman with an even bigger warmth and spirit. Mike told me it was a triumphant day in his life when he could best her at arm wrestling. She frequently says, "It doesn't cost anything to be nice," but when she closed the store during the war she had over ten thousand dollars in uncollected grocery bills. Every once in a while somebody will stop by and give her a ten dollar bill. "My aunt Irene," Mike once said, "is the least anxious person I know."

When Mike's parents got married they converted the second floor of the house into an apartment where Mary operated a beauty shop for many years and where she still lives. Mary will tell me that she has been redecorating, and I feign enthusiasm, knowing she really means that the beige wallpaper flecked with gold has been replaced by mint green flecked with silver. And on these walls she'll restore to their respected prominence the two pictures of the Sacred Heart, three crucifixes, and pictures of saints the church has since defrocked.

We'll park by the hydrant in front of the house, because no one in Whitehall ever gets a ticket. If Rudy, the town's only cop, should be on patrol that night, he'll ring the doorbell and ask Mike to move the car. Rudy is the village homosexual, who is said to have gone straight. He was given the job sort of as a reward for his rehabilitation. I once referred to him as "the fairy fuzz," but he's an accepted part of Whitehall and nobody found my remark very funny. Now I know better.

The front door is never locked and still bears the name of Mike's grandfather, Nicholas Bottiglieri. When we open it fantastic smells fill our nostrils—baking bread, simmering sauce, sauteed veal. Mary will hear us and head for the door. Mary is the puzzle in the picture, the anachronism. Trim, smartly coiffed and made up, wearing a Kimberly knit suit, she might just as easily be descending from a Park Avenue penthouse decorated with Parsons tables and mylar wallpaper. She might, but the events of her life took a different course, and now she rushes to embrace us: my children's noni, my husband's mother, my friend and confidant who asked me to call her "Mary" on that very first visit. "My babies!" she'll say as she hugs the children in a bunch. Then she'll look over our shoulders and say, "Michael, you shouldn't park by the hydrant."

"Don't listen to her, Mike," Irene will say, coming to the door. "Now that she's such a big wheel, she wants us to be law abiding." Mary has just been appointed secretary to the Washington County Family Court.

The children will make a beeline toward the things they have come to count on—a little dish of candy on the table, Irene's Italian cookies heaped on a plate, their baby pictures displayed on top of the piano, the picture in the living room of the grandfather they've never seen. I will make a point to exclaim about the new wallpaper, and Mike will dutifully ask his mother how her new job goes while he feasts on warm, frosted Easter bread. When the children settle down, we'll fix ourselves drinks and sit at the kitchen table. We will cloak ourselves in the strong threads of continuity that seem to offer a warmth and security no success can rival and no money can buy.

*I don't think my mother appreciated the exotic environment she chose for my introduction to prayers. The Liguoris were my first trip away from 117 Broadway. Some of my readers know John Manuel's contrasting experience with the Liguoris, but holy is as holy does. I did learn my prayers and learned to love them. I tried to force the material about prayer into a poem, but the detail was so sharp and overwhelming that conversational prose emerged instead. Here's a trip through the Liguoris' house, prayers and all.*

## PRAYERS

M Y MOTHER LED ME fifty steps from our green asbestos-shingled home to the brown asbestos-shingled house of the Liguoris. This was to be my first educational experience away from home. It turned out to be much further away for me than a few four-year-old steps. It was time to learn my prayers, instructed by the Liguoris.

Since the three women of that household mirrored my grandmother, Innocenta Bottiglieri, my aunt Irene, and my mother Mary, I immediately felt safe and comfortable. Mama Liguori was invariably clothed in a black dress with white polka dots or squares, familiar choices. She was shy compared to my ebullient, extroverted grandmother, who lived downstairs, but they both made wonderful Italian cookies: instant trust.

The two diminutive Liguori daughters were my actual teachers. The whole street was populated with Marys. Mary Liguori was calm, sweet, and supportive. Her sister, Minnie, was crazed by God, or something else, which got her rejected from at least two nunneries. She fervently believed in prayer. In fact, the Liguori women attended each and every religious service held in Our Lady of Angels, the Catholic church on "our side of the crick."

Prayer, done right, is pure emotion. As intense as the learning of prayers was, the most vivid memories were those of the actual tour through the Liguori home. Their front door opened into a dry-cleaning shop, which was their means of temporal support. Rather than incense, I inhaled a bracing draft of dry cleaning fluid, carbon tetrachloride. My lungs immediately belonged to God. The next tiny room plunged me deeply into true devotion. It was dominated by a statue of the Blessed Virgin Mary, another Mary. Clad in blue, she opened her arms to the worshiper. There was a kneeler for prayer, and the room was dimly lit by flickering candles. It was both mystical and creepy. I was gone, totally gone.

Comfort came next, in passage through the commodious kitchen. The nose was beguiled again, this time with aromas of garlic and olive oil. It was a message from Southern Italy challenging the Piedmontese, butter-based cuisine of my home. At last we reached the classroom, a solarium with wicker furniture and large, exotic plants. The palms impressed me the most. However, it was Whitehall, and twenty yards away lay the tracks of the D & H railroad. Our devotions paused as the train thundered by, literally shaking the house, but not our mood of piety.

The sights, the smells, the sounds, and the Liguoris themselves were overwhelming. The prayer, however, was the thing. I was bright, and memorization came quickly and easily. Intoxicated by sensory overload, I was eager to learn. We covered the "Our Father," daily grace, and morning and night prayers. The most intense devotion belonged to the Virgin: "Remember, oh most Blessed Mother, that never was it known that anyone who fled to thy protection, implored thine help, or sought thine intercession, was left unaided," began the "Memorare." It still begins that way.

There was such grandeur in the power of prayer, such comfort in the adoring presence of the women, and such good cookies, that I loved learning my prayers. I was special to them, and we all bought into the Jesus imagery a bit more than was healthy. Most of all, for the first time I felt the power of words, the majesty of meaning, and a sense of transformation. Prayer became the poetry of my childhood, and I am ever grateful.

*Like so much of Whitehall, the reservoir is no more. It has eutrified, become solid ground. No one goes there to talk, swim, smoke, drink, and engage in all the other acts that I, except for the first two, missed. "The Reservoir" was hard to squeeze into poetry and was overlong, which I learned on my first reading in Emily Fragos's poetry workshop at the 92nd Street Y. However, I like the Whitehall lore and refuse to delete what for Emily was tiresome detail. Affection trumps compression every time.*

## THE RESERVOIR

The reservoir occupied high ground
above Whitehall, population 4,000.
To us it was the res'ervoy, not French
but upstate Adirondack diction.
It never was a source of drinking water,
but three to ten boys climbed
to a place that had no rules.

The trail began behind our school,
a red brick box for all twelve grades,
now empty and in disrepair.
We passed the ball field next,
a patch of rocky ground unblessed by grass,
the arena for our class touch football games.

Higher up we went past Bergemeister's Castle.

Only childhood fantasies of knights and courts
could see a castle in the sandstone blocks
scattered randomly about a weedy field.
We failed to see the prophecies
that Whitehall was devolving
into Bergemeister's fate.
The town was tough on grandeur.
Our upward path wound through
forest choked with underbrush and fallen trees.
Chipmunks were the major form of wildlife,
and dead wood's musty scent surrounded us: more decay.

At last we reached the reservoir, ringed
with rocks for chairs. We sat and talked
of Dodgers, Yankees, food, and, haltingly,
of girls. Before us lay welcoming water.
It was hot outside; we'd slip into the cool.
We swam and floated in the pond,
tasting nature at its best.

Touching bottom put an end to pleasure.
The shallow pond was weedy everywhere.
Our reservoir was eutrifying,
choking on proliferating plant life.
My fear arose from standing in the muck and slime,
foot-high weeds attacking ankles
like some sin from down below.
Panic shouted, "Swim like mad, escape!"
But no one else seemed frightened, and

no one said, "Watch out for deadly mire!"
The reservoir was not the place for me to buckle
under nature's benthic demons.
Surrender was no option.
It was cool, and so were we.

Happiness was living on the surface, floating free.
Keep your feet up off the bottom —
nothing good arises from beneath.

*I really did gather thousands of earthworms for fishing. My father, Uncle John, Aunt Irene, and I were the main pickers. We would drench the front lawn in the evening to suffocate the worms and drive them to the surface. Then we would pick them in the near dark. If we didn't, we would have to purchase them from Juckett's Bait Shop, which was as disgusting as the Liguoris' was spiritual. Incidentally, several other poets (Diane Lockward, Billy Collins, and John Updike) have tackled earthworms.*

## NIGHTCRAWLERS

On cool wet summer nights the crawlers,
emissaries from the earth,
lie strewn  like lazy matchsticks,
basking in the starlight.

The worm is cautious, and one end
stays anchored to his hole.
In his small world: he's no one's fool.

This is a quest for a moonlit boy,
picking worms and dropping them in large tin pails,
then bending them to his own purpose.
The sharp-eyed hunter strikes!
Fingers flash down at the hole,
for worms are far too quick
for grasping at the end you see.

A catch! The rough rings of the worm
contract in desperation.
Half in, half out, he grasps his hole.
Don't yank, he'll break. You'll have
two worms too small for bait.
Pull gently, firmly, till his grip releases.
You are then his keeper.

One hunt's a prelude to the next,
with crawlers in the temptress role.
First jab the hook straight
through the worm's thick collar,
then bind the worm up twice more to the barb.
Spasms wrack the worm.
His contortions flood the hands
with sticky slime, his last resistance.

Into the lake the worm is tossed,
accompanied by bob and sinker.
Out of sight Salome writhes,
beckoning pike and pumpkinseed.
This dance is played beneath the glass.
A tug, a flick of rod, and careful play
brings up a silver trophy for the boy,
scaling the food chain from earth
to water to the fisherman.

*Nothing about Whitehall would be complete without the presence of Aunt Irene. You had to know her. If any person was a force of nature and a fountain of good will, it was Aunt Irene. She also loved colorful language and salty metaphors, which I still cherish. How could "busier than a one-armed paper hanger" be more descriptive?*

## AUNT IRENE

My aunt Irene ruled from the stove,
serving food and love with pungent verse
and deep contempt for formal niceties.
She filtered life through bawdy wit
and served it hot and fresh.

"What's for dinner?" I would ask.
"Horseshit and bread.

What do you want first?"
These were her metaphors:
"Flatter than a plate of piss.
Plainer than a duck's ass.
Colder than a witch's tit.
Hotter than Dutch love."

Those disrespected were
"Ten pounds of shit
In a five pound bag," or
"He wouldn't say shit if
he had a mouthful."
"Mike, Mike, strike a light,
the baby shit a worm"
baffled me when six years old.
Now it's thirty years too late
to ask her what it meant.

Irene's words, her caring and her food,
created an entirely singular admixture.
But then, at times, it's hard to tell
the fly shit from the pepper
in the crystal shaker.

# Part Two:
# My Life

*Poets sketch nature, struggle with words, and are always seeking new perceptions. Most of all, they like to write about themselves. Here are five poems about my life. Two are humorous, two poignant, and one is a bit of both.*

*My first memory is, indeed, that of my first lie, or at least the first I can remember. At what age do you recall telling your first lie? I seem to have developed the knack early. Eric Erickson said that our first lie demarcates us from the rest of the world. Pretty scary, but we all have our lies. "Lies" has been useful in reminding me of my patients' ubiquitous conflicts over truth.*

## LIES

My first memory is my first lie,
a needle piercing through my childhood,
opening the course for legions more to come.
My mother told me not to play that game indoors,
but I wanted to and threw the wooden ball
that cracked the glass door of the cupboard.
A boy of three, I felt a flood of fear and shame—
not remorse, but "What will my mother say?"
In my desperation I lied, the template for the tide to come.
She knew and softly chided me.

My father told me not to play with fire.
Fathers give such warnings: sons disobey.
The fire flared inside an old oil drum

and I, nine-year-old moth, reached out to touch it.
When I pulled my blistered hand away,
the rising bubble instantly betrayed my deed.
I had been bad and I bore that mark of shame.
Again I lied. "I was running and my hand flew out.
It was an accident I touched the fire."
He hit me, rather gently, for the first and only time.
The greater pain was disappointing him.

For forty years of adulthood I struggled
with ancient enemies, my weakness and my shame.
Not about illicit sexual adventures,
or even cheating on a test or taxes:
it's not the magnitude of lies that matter.
It's the same sad structure of deceit
erected in that fateful third year.
To my loving wife I swore
that I had given smoking up, or soon would.
One more blot, and more the shame for me, a doctor.

They've disappeared now—my mother, father, cigarettes.
Well, at times, the last sends up a twitch
of hunger ( I cannot lie).
Give me one more bit of self-indulgence.
Who, indeed, would catch me now?
Gone are all those lies that wove the chain
of shame and secrecy, and of self-hatred.
Gone, too, the threat of truth and exposure.
The credit, sadly, goes to age and withered pride.

I'd celebrate the waning of my flaws,
except I see myself upon my deathbed,
surrounded by my loved ones, saying to them,
"No, it's not so bad, don't worry."
One last lie.

*"I Became a Doctor" recalls observing my father's near death when I was eleven years old. "Loss," which follows directly, is about the lasting impact of his death three years later. The feelings are still with me. I found that when I had only one remaining parent, I needed another for stability. Work became, and still is, my proxy father, with many attendant consequences.*

*It took me fifty five years to write or talk openly about these experiences, but every time I recite these poems, I feel a little lighter. Read aloud, they have been as healing as four and a half years of psychoanalysis, when I talked about little else. They are my first and most important lessons in the power of poetry.*

## I BECAME A DOCTOR

As my eleventh year was ending,
I stood silent in my bedroom, watching,
shaken by the nightlong struggle
of my father in the vestibule of death.

While the doctor worked to save his life,
I looked on from one to five AM.
This is what I saw:

> purple lips and mottled skin,
> rasping sounds of labored breathing,
> fluid bubbling from his mouth,
> eyes rolled back and semiconscious,
> bruises where the doctor drew
> > huge vials of blood to bring his pressure down.

Though he lived three years beyond that crisis,
not yet twelve, I knew
Our time together would be brief.
Through that night I chewed the hated cud of helplessness.
Neither could I swallow it nor could I spit it out.
At dawn I slept, a child, awakening to be a doctor.
Then I learned new words describing what I'd seen:

> cyanosis,
> dyspnea,
> pulmonary edema,
> phlebotomy,
> purpura.

Strange that merely different names
bring me comfort, but they do.
Words are simply kinder than the pictures.

# LOSS

I've borne a loss for fifty years,
 in a silent, hidden space
with room for only me
and for my long-dead shadow.
The burden comes in many ways,
but mostly in the stubborn, dogged
need for goodness, camouflaged as work.
So gripped, I stumble through my days
of numbing toil, the secret sore inside.

He didn't choose it, nor did I.
If he had seen, could he have spoken words
that I, at fourteen, could have grasped?
And who could see the soul transformed,
laced with guilt and obligation?
The hardest part is debt unpaid,
the ledger closed too soon
and I forever in the red.

*"Me And Sean" returns to the wonderful things in life: playing poker, having kids, and marrying a loving partner who enabled both. Sean, my son, suggested this adventure during our LBI vacation. Our first trip to Atlantic City resulted in this poem, and the second trip led to a third place finish in a formidable Texas Hold'Em tournament. I can still wheel and deal 'em. Maureen got Italy, Ed got college night, Tim got the Super Bowl, but Sean got the poem. The title leads directly into the poem, a device I learned from Ted Kooser's* The Poetry Home Repair Manual. *The language is pure pokerese.*

## ME AND SEAN

Went to AC, his call, to wage the wars of Texas Hold'Em:
a father / son thing.
Ten men, four old and six young bucks,
surround a battlefield of green.
Eyes downcast, codgers count their chips.
Stacks rise like hopes of being at the final table.
Stacks shrink like hearts they hoped would flush
but ended clubbed to death, a burial by spades,
or was it diamonds?

The young men look the part— dark glasses, backward caps,
twirling chips with just one hand.
Tonight they worship Jesus Ferguson and Moneymaker,

neither God nor Mammon, but current TV poker pros.
They bust and drift to playing three and six, or two and four,
the purgatory of their broken dreams.
Fifth hand, Sean draws a nutted flush and goes all in.
Good move.
He busts against a boat drawn on the river.
Poker luck.                                                             20.


And I, the aged rookie, play it tight,
scratching out two careful hours
only to be done in by the rising blinds.
This duel is suited only for the young and bold.
The games I played were different:

> Five Card Stud and Down The River
> Dr. Jack Sorbetter
> Guts
> High-Low
> Chicago
> Omaha
> Anaconda
> Baseball (Day and Night)
> One Eyed Jacks, The Man With The Axe
>         and A Pair of Natural 7's Wild
> Doctor Pepper (With A Pepper Checker)
> The Old Rugged Cross
> And my favorites, Panic and Panic In The Streets.

Tired of checks, of folds and raises, and of lying in the weeds,

we move from lights to night.
A battered lady of the trade, recently thrown from a car,
tempts Sean—for a modest price.
Another AC moment.
"Thanks a lot, but we've already lost enough."
To Donald Trump, to Meyer Lansky,
to Wynn and all the captains of casino greed, I tip my hat.
Me and Sean had a blast that night
in the garish sandbox of the Taj Mahal.

—8/8/06  (The AC night)

*When I told my mother I had been asked to comment on a New York
Times article on procrastination, she said, "Well, Michael, they certainly
chose the right person." Here's to that special sickening feeling of guilt we
have all felt as the Sunday night syndrome unfolds.*

## SUNDAY EVENING, 6 :10 PM

The sky
is thick
with chickens
coming home
to roost —
on me.

# Part Three:
# Our Love

*When you find the right person, loving for a lifetime is easy. Writing about it is hard. These three poems from Patty and me are gifts to one another, so please treat them gently. The first poem is a remembrance of a brief but unforgettable spontaneous moment after dinner with Katy and Terry in their Greenwich Village loft.*

## EAST TENTH STREET
*(To Pat)*

Looking for the car,
walking down East Tenth,
soaking up the hot
night air, swollen with
the music of New York

were we touched by wit,
the crisp white chardonnay,
or was it merely
moonlight coursing over
midnight lovers?

It might have pushed up
molten from the Earth's
core into ours, deaf
to passing cabs, blind
to shuttered storefronts.

Or was there special
softness brushing up
against each other;
starfall dancing blond
on beauty's canvas?

No sense to question
gravity, or ask
why every sky is
blue—fevered passion
bartered words for song.

We pressed against brick
wall, mingling sudden
soft with hard, slow with
quick, our hands gliding
through the veils of cloth.

Who knew desire could
 burn so deeply
that the feel, the taste
of East Tenth lives today,
forty years later.

*The next poem, deeply heartfelt, came on an insomniac night at Tim and Sue's. Once the poem was started, I couldn't sleep from the excitement of its meaning. It was my gift to Patty. The second poem that follows is her next day response. It is really intense.*

## I'D LIKE TO LEAVE YOU

I'd like to leave you
music, laughing children,
beads of passion
strung through time,
beach days, and memories
of a beautiful life spent together.

I'd like to leave you
knowing, as a wife,
your care, your wit,
your words and intimacies,
and, yes, your pilgrim soul has
been my steel, my soufflé, my life.

I'd like to leave you
saying no one,
no thing, no love
that I'd imagined
could approach that
which you've brought to us.

## TO MIKE

If you were to leave me

The beach would burn,
The wine would choke,
I couldn't sing,
And I would cling
Like a mad woman to your ashes,
Or jump into your grave.
The children couldn't stop me.

—*Patty*

*Part Four:*
*Medical Poems*

*Being a doctor for forty-six years generates lots of memories. Oddly, my years of doing psychotherapy haven't made it into poetry yet. This poem recalls one of my first experiences as an intern. The memory wouldn't go away and I didn't know what to do with it. Eventually it became a poem, where it rests.*

## MEMENTO MORI

The first one caught me by surprise.

I was doing my initial thoracentesis,
a task less daunting than the word implies.
A cheerful woman gasped from fluid in her chest,
a pleural effusion caused by rampant cancer.
There was no effusiveness in the somber needle
I guided carefully through her chest wall.
"I'm going to die now," she said calmly,
and, with nothing further, lay back dead.

It was the moment doctors fear;
full frontal with the enemy ahead,
and I midwife to the highest drama.
This was no time for contemplation.
Coding, CPR, intracardiac adrenaline—
we were quick and forceful, but for nothing.
Relatives were notified, and in intense detail
we probed each second, searching for a clue or cause.

None came, and nothing from a later autopsy.
We had no solution, no solace, no one to blame.

While preachers celebrate the rising soul,
and mystics sense transfiguration, and
loved ones clasp one another, casting
hope against the loneliness of death,
we found no answer in her body,
no meaning in the metaphysics,
and nothing in ourselves to talk about.

*The next poem, "Callous", is the first one I wrote as an adult. It has been described as "depraved" and "disgusting," and vilified in even stronger terms. The inspiration, "Sunday Morning," by Wallace Stevens, is one of our greatest American poems. Read the first few stanzas of his poem to set the focus on loss of the sacred. It's online.*

*One Sunday morning, well after I had replaced church attendance with foot care, I had just read Stevens, and the poem came to me; church, calloused feet, and Wallace Stevens. My podiatrist offered to try and get it published in the American Journal of Podiatry. Shamelessly, I said, "Okay." Pat asked me why I added the "u" in callous and I said it was the British spelling. "Oh," she said, "the British Journal of Podiatry." It is still seeking publication— anywhere.*

*The poem itself is modern, i.e., without rhymes or strict formal structure. It has a lot going on, weaving together disparate experiences, wordplay, double meanings, and irony. The only connection with medicine is its focus on a body part. Poets, in general, like the poem; most readers, not so much.*

## CALLOUS

*(For Wallace Stevens's "Sunday Morning")*

When steel meets flesh, the outcome
should be no surprise: rasp versus corn.
The steel is sharp and new and peels off layers

of the old.  Keratin, encasing sole,
offers no resistance.
Should I slip or scrape too deep,
the hidden world beneath the shell
emerges pink and painful.
Stung by air, it oozes knowledge
of an inner-dwelling life.

My Sunday rites are now such doings:
coffee, papers, shower, smoothing of the feet.
There used to be a deeper, different call
of Latin, incense, and the scab of sin
to pick at on the day of rest.
Now mystery is lost,
and mundane chores of filing fill the void
of aging hope and lost faith.
But, lacking gods, the question stands:
"Does dead skin shield my soul?"

The hoof of man, which fell
so pliant to the Sunday file,
regenerates, breeds more hard skin, in time
erodes the steel and leaves it
smooth and  helpless, futile.
The pink rests safe beneath its shield.
The body is the harder jewel.
The soul that promised immortality,
encased with ease, slumbers
soft, contented, blesséd.

*"Serum" is my second "medical" poem loosely based on body parts. Like most of the ensuing "medical poems," the subtext is hubris. The constituency of the serum of our blood is almost identical to sea water. Our body regulates the balance of electrolytes in serum rigorously. I like the fact that we are walking bags of sea water. It says something about evolution. The ending is green, but the BP spill hints that reconciliation may be a long way off.*

## SERUM: THE SEA WITHIN

We ought to love the ocean
without whose womb we would not be.
The thickened sea that fills our veins
proclaims its parentage.
Its chemistry surrounds our every cell.
Our body matches bloody brine
in perfect measure with the sea.
Our heartbeat, pressures, respiration,
all have lives of individuality and change.
They fluctuate.  Our saltiness does not, can not.

Our lives are merely episodes
borrowed from an ancient Triton
who long ago stopped caring for his children.
Who, out of curiosity or simple carelessness,
set us free, forgot to stop our evolution
before we left our birthplace

and abused our old aquatic ancestry.
Perhaps some day that oneness will return
to us who see ourselves as
separate, self-determined, ordained to rule the waves:
a modest reconciliation of our substance
with its genesis, a saline sisterhood  and
salty kinship with the creatures of the sea.

*It's pushing the edge to poeticize my time in the womb. However, it is anatomic, at least in name, and anything is grist for a poem.*

## THE WOMB

I found a crack in unbeing
and, wedged within  a shell,
was borne by viscous liquid
in communion with another.
I liked the ease,
the lack of obligation,
the sense of being part of something
larger, better, more caring,
and yet still me.

Yes, I recall the womb,
the softness felt
pressing at its gentle borders.
Every hour I changed

my axis, exploring
supple, unseen boundaries.
I stretched; like honey,
resistance sweetly filled
each void I made.

I had no breath
and yet I breathed.
Substance filled my lungs,
sustaining me in my airless vault.
I had no voice,
but everything I needed came to me.
I had no sight,
but knew my crimson mantle
was world enough for then.

Nothing since has ever felt
and fit like God's completeness.


*The next four poems are loosely based on the special senses. "Vision" is a riff on the phenomenon that many newborns have vascularized corneas, impairing their sight. The science is approximate, invoking poetic license. The more humor, the more rhyme. Modern poetry editors seem to hate rhyme, but sometimes it just happens.*

## VISION

Science calls it maturation,
a simple fact of no great mind,
that infants feel before they see,
brothers, sisters, all born blind.

Should we fear the doctor's dictum?

That blindness has no meaning
confounds our sense of human worth.
And so we struggle to uncover
importance in this quirk of birth—

and spurn the role of nature's victim.

Or is it merciful indulgence,
to spare a child the social traces
that force the newly born to smile
at recognition of our faces,

a brief vacation at the start of life?

Can the infant born in darkness,
feeling first the warmth and chills,
start to nurse apart from vision,
guided by inherent skills?

Will it last through later strife?

Dark recalls the peace and comfort
of our lost protected place.
Fetal feeding came so freely,
tied to mother's giving grace.

Do we lose it as we grow?

Seeing starts the fledgling matrix
kindling thoughts of what will be.
Darkness leads us back to ponder —
have we known eternity?

Do we really want to know?

When we find the second blindness
is it anguish of the cursed,
or a song of reconciling,
like the music of the first?

Could we bear to see such light?

Life is many muddled circles,
history of men gone wild
seeking to regain the wisdom
of the sightless newborn child.

Let me learn to love the night.

*The rhyming in "Smell" gets out of control in the second half of the poem, with internal and ending rhymes. Lots of rhyme leads to doggerel, and I like that development here. My college honors thesis was written on Naturphilosophie, an obscure nineteenth-century school of German philosophy of science based on the medieval concept of a Great Chain of Being. Ockenfuss, the nature philosopher, could have used a little humor and more modesty about man's superiority to "lower" animals. There is an honorary note in the final stanza for CJ, our beloved family dog.*

## SMELL

One thousand years ago, the pious monks,
betrothed to God alone, rapt with Gregorian,
thinking of the role of nature's creatures,
perceived a Chain of Being topped by man.

The rule of natural law was clear:
 mankind had unquestioned place
above all others, for his image
traced the lines of God's own face.

From there  the chain descended—
apes, birds, fish, and sundry forms —
an order unsurprising, since mankind,
the king, had set its norms.

The soul aside, the monks decried,
"What keeps man at the zenith,
is speech and prayer, God's gift to sayer,
who speaketh what he meaneth."

Our brain is twain, but, in the main,
the part that serves our species well
is most profound with sight and sound,
but comes up short on smell.

We do not seek out those who reek,
but give them ample berth.
If cleanliness is godliness,
then lack of smell is worth.

In contrast, dogs, like backward gods,
occupy a lower tier.
However, smell does serve them well,
despite connection to their rear.

To love or hate, to bark or mate,
are issues of posterior.
But who's to say, though try we may,
that our way is superior?

Let's put aside our sense of pride.
In scents we can't compete
with dogs, a strain who humbly deign
to lick our smelly feet.

*"Hearing" got published because it appealed to the poetry editor of The Pharos, a journal with social and cultural themes related to medicine. This poem, like almost all of "Medical Poems," turns on hubris. Ambrose Gilligan, my seventh-grade science teacher, annoyed me with the formal definition of sound. I knew something was wrong with it, but he wouldn't back down despite my arguments. Here's my revenge.*

## HEARING

In seventh grade my teacher said,
"If no man hears, there is no sound."
What of the honking goose, the howling wolf?
Does human absence still their voices, make them mute?

How like ourselves to hear a world
defined by just our presence.
Somewhere an ancient elm falls dead.
Honor its demise.  Grant that it too makes a sound.

*This poem, a play on words, taught me how difficult it is to write a Shakesperean sonnet. The result shows. I haven't gotten the touch yet, nor do I have a poem about the fifth sense, touch. Again, it's more about the word and less about the sensory gift. It's as close as I will ever come to Elizabethan sentiment.*

## TASTE

To be born full of grace, bountiful charm
to shine on old or pretty women, would
be a miracle of Sutric karma,
flowers growing riot in pine green wood.
If we start instead with innate taste,
restrained, directed at timeless beauty,
vermillion strands in golden robes so chaste
that adoration comes from mere duty,
then these gifts would vie against each other.
Charity restrains mean-spirited fight.
Charm and taste should be like brothers,
though the former casts a brighter light.
Still I'd count my pretty manners, false and true,
and sacrifice them for one taste of you.

# Part Five:
# Art

*It's time to get wordy about art; Pat and I have followed avante-garde art since the mid-sixties. The art movements have aged along with us, but we've never lost interest and still love afternoons in Chelsea. This is one of my best poems, and the first published. Every word counts, making the poem appropriate for minimalism. Compression is the poet's holy grail. Less is more if you do it right. Google the artists for the best appreciation of the poem. It's about them.*

## MINIMALISM

If I could write like Robert Ryman paints,
    I'd write in white
    on white,
    with hues so slight
that meaning would be whispers.

If I could write like James Turrell sculpts,
    I'd write with air
    and forms so spare
    that in and out would both be bare,
and substance would be light.

If I could write like Philip Glass composes,
    I'd take an ordinary sound
    and turn it round
    and round and round
until its echoes glistened.

*Conceptualism is one of the least recognized postmodern art movements. It first grabbed me with Bruce Nauman's triptich:*

| TAR | ART | RAT |

*Nauman said, "I think the point where language starts to break down as a useful tool for communication is the edge where poetry and art occurs." Pretty deep. This poem about conceptualism includes a conceptual painting, in disguise, within the poem itself. Find it. That's a lot of words about a poem, but conceptualists like both the forms of letters and enigmatic humor. The poetry and the art are hard to digest, and a plethora of words is usually the introduction to a flawed poem.*

## CONCEPTUALISM

Color, sensate succubus,
esthetic whore, seduces our
wit and judgment.  It stirs
retinal concupiscence
and leaves us in post-coital torpor.
Resist, find rational intelligence.
Rise higher. Shout
      NO, TART!

Should we slip these wiles,
Odysseus beseiged by ocular
sirens, then content next
beguiles us with the fleshy wench,
realism, and the wicked lure of form.
Still, resist temptation,
find intellectual restraint.  Proclaim
                    NO, TART!


We embrace the purest concept,
words and the grace of letters.
We take translucent thought and
transcendent wit unfiltered.
We reject the silky slut of surface and
embrace the clarity, the words themselves.
We murmur to our modern mate,
                    ART!

*Poets are notoriously crossover artists, always fishing in several ponds. I have always struggled to get more poetry into my poetry, and this is a frontal assault , conflating poetry with the language of music and painting. Like much self-conscious poetry, it revels in big words and is somewhat pretentious.*

## SCRATCH A POET

Scratch a poet, most bleed music.
Scratch a poet, some bleed paint.
Meter plays as  green crescendo,
rhyme speaks in a blue sforzando.
Poems are translucent bottles
shaping lines of red glissando,
some emboldened, others faint.

Muddied tones and scumbled chords,
symphonies of chromic words,
sonnets mounted on a grid,
make counterpoint of imagery.
Love and death, the poet's treasures,
sculpted into written measures,
grow from  inner harmony.

Twenty-six first cousins mingle,

joining with the eighty-eight
to dance the arc of ROY G BIV.
Try to hide the inner music,
vivid hues inspiring verse,
skeletons from  kindred arts.
Poetry is just the face.

# Part Six: Humor

*Humor in poetry is as difficult to convey as love. This is, and probably will always be, my briefest poem. They don't get much more succinct.*

## MY NEW WHITE SNEAKERS

are squeaky
and geeky.

*I've had a lot of fun with the following six lines. Restaurant recitations have a captured, if not a captivated audience. Sometimes it's good for a piece of cake, too.*

## FOIE GRAS

There ought to be a *loi*
to punish those who eat *foie gras*.
Whose conscience, so *sauvage*,
permits them the *gavage*
of poor, defenseless goose,
to make a trendy *amuse bouche*.

*Here's my poetic homage to the MacMahons, Patty's family, who tried to teach me to tremble at the beach. I was a novice, and Mac instructed me about ocean technique while Peg provided whimsical advice. I've now had ocean worries in seven states, and I always watch the waves. The MacMahons were good teachers, and Patty provides continuing reinforcement. The poem is tongue in cheek.*

## ENJOY THE BEACH

but never take your eyes
off the ocean waves.
Crashing surf tosses you
and breaks your bones
unless you bob or duck...
at just the proper time.
Facing shoreward lets
the unseen surf  behind
attack.  Breaths are short,
balance lost, and shells and
rocks and sand abrade you.
Safety first,

and watch for deadly rip tides,
undercurrents pulling
out to sea.  Can you
fight your way back in?

No, you'll tire and sink
against relentless force.
Rips flow to extinction
out one hundred yards or so.
Ride them like a cloud.
Drift to safety in their
effortless embrace.
Keep your head,

and always have a sharp eye
out for little children
sweeping out to sea.
Parents aren't always
what they ought to be.
Keep your strong hands ready
to pluck the helpless tots
from the boiling surf.
Be a hero, and
enjoy the beach.

"Radio Ball" is a piece of nostalgia from childhood Whitehall nights listening to the Brooklyn Dodgers on the radio. Even then I didn't like the Yankees.

## RADIO BALL

Watching  baseball on the radio,
where every contest is a home game
played on the wrinkled gray surface
of my brain, is time condensed
into many a hot summer night.
The slider, low and away, the
6-4-3 double play, and the bunt
still leap from the airwaves,
spin into my mind, and shine
with metaphysical clarity.

Between plays, announcers talk
of movies, restaurants, stats,
players' quirks, and stats, stats, stats.
Their banter, verbal foul balls out of play,
never make it into the box score.
Not everything can be recorded,
but seventy years of memories
blend sound  and sight without error.
Best: Time is slow, and I could live
forever in the game of radio ball.

# Part Seven:
## Ideas

*My friend Irving Sandrof was a composer of univocal lipograms, poems using only one vowel. Charles Simic is a past poet laureate. When I put timid in front of Simic the "I's" marched across the page. Its an homage to both men and looks better than it sounds.*

## I TIMID SIMIC

I, timid Simic,
fight insipid writing.
Bristling, finding limits,
I bring limpid light, insight.

King Irving, Simic, Vikings
lighting mighty nights —
singing fists, vivid wisps,
glimpsing rhyming flights.

Bring Simic's mythic spin,
stir spirits blind within.
Finding right, binding sin,
high signs, my rising kin.

*Here is a quirky, loosely scientific, bizarre poem. The comparison of the gyre in an emptying basin to sexual release came from somewhere I have never travelled. The next leap to cosmic destruction and reunion is equally baffling and totally over the top. The poem comes in six stanzas of six lines.*

## THE GYRE

This basin flat with water,
motionless, finds life
with just the pulling of a plug.
Then starts the dance of drainage,
where circles move with the clock,
or against it if in Rio.

A gyre is formed. At first in contact with walls,
it circles slowly, then gains vigor.
Always focused inward, it moves faster,
deeper, tighter; then  plunges into nowhere.
It leaves no sound or trace,
submitting to gravity's attraction.

Human passion hides beneath a different surface,
its power cloaked by work and obligation.
It opens to the strains of sensuality:
a flash of skirt, the gentle curve of breasts,
muscled arms, pulsating rhythm,
or just the memory of turnings past.

This circle, too, starts out centripetal and slow.
At first in contact with the world,
it swirls inward ever faster, tighter, deeper,
consuming space between the lover and the other.
Apart from time or will, this gyre implodes,
its echoes those of peace and solitude.

Our universe, all that we know and see,
exploded from a ball of energy
some fourteen billion years ago.
It now flies outward, spewing stars,
spawning dreams of endless space to fill,
and we the keepers of its history.

But here and there we see again the gyre,
black holes that rotate, stars that disappear,
victims of unseen forces.
When what we know, our universe,
begins to twist and spin, the next great gyre
will make a new community of you and me.

*"Visitors" has an art and poetry reference, but it's really just something exceptional that happened for only seconds.*

## VISITORS

This was no exaltation of larks, merely
a hundred starlings swarming to sit
on my  winter bare backyard sycamore,
arranging themselves in careful spacings,
patterns that would please a Sol LeWitt.

They came to roost as one,
their rationale too deep to glean.
Were they united, of one mind,
or merely airborne sheep,
 not brave enough to fly alone?

There are no thirteen ways of looking
at these blackbirds,  only one,
and that infused with nature's oddity.
The cloud of black ascends again to sky,
soaring out of sight and into memory.

*One spring day on the way to Pelham, New York, Patty pointed out to me the reddish hue of bare woods covered with leaf buds. The poem came that night, and the rhyming made its way in at the very end. The idea of spring as the destroyer tickled me. This poem, like a few others, has balanced stanzas, in this case, of ten lines each.*

## LATE MARCH, NORTHERN NEW JERSEY

Rust red the March wood stands.
Not sea, but seeds that bulge
on restless, twig-brown hands.
Not scarlet, crimson,
shades that shout, "Now. See."
Viridian, the red with earth
within, by day is dance played free
against background of blue.
Warm, cool,  the buds and sky
perform a minuet a due.


The wind, now soft, now harsh,
quixotic master facing March,
shakes buds into a tremor.
The sense of it eludes me.
Did red make March alive?

Is nature mocking pewter skies
of months just past, or calling forth
bright days for coming exercise?
Is she extracting laughs from cries
or flights of birds from skidding cars?

How cruelly comes pale petal green,
announcing red's demise.
Am I the only one who sees what dies?
Barrenness, abstraction,
my winter observations,
are fast devoured by flames of green,
the lemon green of resurrection.
Of cold, and husk, and then rebirth,
the middle is least often seen—
except for glimpses in late March.

# Part Eight:
# Light and Dark

*Jon Long pointed out that light and dark are motifs in much of my po-etry. Along with "Vision," the last four poems revolve around light and dark and have an ironic sensibility. Light and dark as life and death? I guess so.*

*We were staying at our friends the Enziens' lake house. The morning light, the calm water, the cool temperature, and being relaxed and alone were the perfect backdrop for a bitter poem. The paradoxical tone of the poem surprised me. Again, hammering out a sonnet proved to be a chore. This one is a bit more successful than its predecessor, "Taste."*

## BE YOURSELF

Dawn, a muttering day of disposal,
a weary wind blowing sour in my face,
this ten-hour trudge, a dour proposal
for lifeless pursuit; all scrapple, no grace.
Children of sight should struggle, obliquely,
defy narcosis, the pull to conform.
Children of night should never go meekly,
ornaments, furbelow, slaves to the norm.
Sunshine noon altared leaches my passion,
bleaching the lunatic colors of lust;
Money becomes our workaday ration,
America's motto, "In God We Trust."
Daylight, the host of a comfortable squalor,
shows in each day, another damn dollar.

*This is an early poem and a favorite. It is a ballad with iambs of*
   *ta da  ta da  ta da  ta da*
      *ta da  ta da  ta da ...*
*Keeping the rhythm is crucial, and fitting every word into four and*
*three alternating iambs is the drill. Brevity is an additional virtue. It reads*
*well aloud.*


## SUNSHINE


The reason I hate sunshine is
   it comes from just one source,
while darkness finds us everywhere
   and softly runs its course.

It merges with our solitude,
   like nature's healing force.
The sun is cruel, and shows us as
   we are, without remorse.


*When you start writing poetry after age sixty-five, dusk is bound to be-*
*come a theme. Light and dark epitomize change, and are with us until we*
*are no longer with them. Crepuscular animals are most active in twilight,*
*i.e., the times between day and night.*

## DUSK

Crepuscular animals
live in three realms;
one foot in daylight,
one  in night, and
the rest in transition.

Owls arouse to feed
on fleeing field mice.
Deer forage at dusk,
their eyes luminous
in my headlights.
Trout, in their habitat,
covet rising mayflies
dancing in  the waning light.

These creatures celebrate
dusk, while, at seventy,
a shadow grows inside  me.
Fading taste and hearing,
hardened corneas,
and mental misfires
hint at dimming times.
Dusk ushers every
daylight to its end.

Coming to the end of my book was problematic. So let's end with a bang, the ending of the universe. Once the idea of heaven lost its credibility, I needed a new myth to give me hope of seeing lost loved ones again. This is it, the wheel of time.

Like "The Gyre," the science is approximate, but we are electrons, tiny clouds of probability ( Heisenberg) held together for too brief a time. Is the universe a giant yo-yo? Will I perceive, in any way, the billion billion billion billionth of a second when everything collapses to be one once again?

The theme and the rhyme make this poem a favorite of mine. It resonates with the sense of loss, but ends in reunion and rebirth. The ending is a beginning. Nice, if doubtful.

## MANDALA

So everybody dies, I think. A blink
of time divides this living state
from that which knows no time or date.
And death can give us cause for dread
if loneliness lies up ahead.
The afterlife aside, we all abide
as tiny clouds of probability,
drifting through infinity,
electrons in immensity.

I'd like to rub against Pascal
and probe his Christian rationale.
And Buddha, does he float? I note
in time I'll meet the endless blur,
the alphabet of all who were,
random travelers in the dark,
bumping in this Noah's Ark
of space…
a trace
of every thing in every place.

A tiny ball began it all.
For fourteen billion years we've flown apart,
the ending as unsure as Big Bang's start.
Still, we try to leaven
grief and loss with hopes of heaven.
And if an afterlife's a hoax,

the joke's not on us yet.
The universe collapsing will, in time, beget
return to matter's primal set.

And sweet will be
the density
of you and me.

## ABOUT THE AUTHOR

Michael R. Milano, M.D., has practiced psychiatry and lived in Teaneck, New Jersey, for forty years. He started life in the small upstate New York village of Whitehall, where he was nurtured by a large extended Italian family, which provided him with a rich store of characters and experiences that appear in many of his poems.

From Whitehall his life took a radical departure into the intellectual and cultural world of Harvard University, where he played poker, met his wife, Pat, and did a pre-med major in the history of science. This was followed by medical school, psychiatry residency, and a tour in the army. Questions emanating from these years can be seen in a series of his poems. Dr. Milano has a rich and vibrant family, social, and athletic life. He is an avid golfer, tennis player, and award-winning amateur winemaker. He and his wife have four children and six grandchildren, a large extended family, and an extensive network of friends who, he hopes, will enjoy his poetry.

This book has been set in Perpetua, designed by Eric Gill in the early part of the 20th century; he based it on the designs of old engravings. His most popular Roman typeface, it was released by the Monotype Corporation between 1925 and 1932, first appearing in a limited edition of the book *The Passion of Perpetua and Felicity*, for which the typeface was named. The italic form was originally called Felicity. The formal impression which this font lends to any text is due in part to its small, diagonal serifs and its medieval numbers.

LaVergne, TN USA
27 January 2011
214324LV00002BB/65/P